The Silent Advocate

M.M. Bylo

Copyright © 2021 by M.M. Bylo

All rights reserved. No part of this book may be reproduced or used in any manner without written permission of the copyright owner except for the use of quotations in a book review.

To request permission, contact the copyright owner at
marissabylo@gmail.com

First edition September 2021
Cover design by Haley Lambert
ISBN: 978-0-578-96144-6

www.mmbylo.com
marissabylo@gmail.com

To you who thought, believed, and lived out the lies. Remember that you are lovely and to live.

To you who haven't found your voice yet. I'll keep making noise until you find the words and strength for yourself.

To you.

I'll see you in the morning ;

Contents

I. The Belittling

2	Soliloquy: Word Assassination
3	An Extrovert Who Developed Social Anxiety, An Apology
5	The Good Girl's Confession
6	Weird
7	Mosaic
8	Archetype
10	I Am Your Sunshine
11	The Silent Advocate
12	They Wrote In Report Cards "She Has Leadership Qualities"
13	Alcoholism Runs In The Family
15	Repress
16	Broken Signals
18	Dysfunctional Empathy
19	Punishment
20	Gaslighting

II. Aftermath

22	Nonstop
23	Mania?
25	I Got That Warm Weather Optimism
27	The World Is My Stage
29	Self-Mandated Quarantine
31	SAD
32	Little Woman
33	Stigma
35	Dreamer's Slumber
37	Unscripted
39	Intermission: A Panic Attack Waiting In The Wings

Contents

III. Regrowth

41   Keep Face
43   Enneagram Type 2, Translation: Low-Key Codependency
44   Insecure
45   Driftwood
46   Call Declined
48   Defiance
50   Deceptive Comfort
52   Tender Heart
53   Little One
55   Canvas
56   Epilogue: Honeycomb Affirmations

Part I
The Belittling

Little One
You silently suffer
But no one is fooled anymore
Be honest with yourself
Who is it that silenced you?

Soliloquy: Word Assassination

Words paint my World

Soar
Dream
Achieve
                    Small

Descend
Levitate
Reminisce
                    Prude

Drift
Confliction
Apathy
                    Weird

Isolate
Lonesome
Phantom
                    Sensitive

Sink
Sabotage
Shatter
                    Burden

Bury
Inevitable
Shame
                    Unlovable

That word
I always forget
Dissociate
         So, who am I now…

An Extrovert Who Developed Social Anxiety, An Apology

After pleasantries about the weather
You ask about me
Since I've never been one for small talk
Please understand
You brought this on yourself

Ahem...

Yes, I've been this height since twelve
A feature everyone fixates on
Do not hesitate to ask if I am old enough
To drive, buy liquor, or grocery shop

PSA: Seasonal Affective Disorder exists
Behold the poster child
A five-foot small high school freshman
First experience circa 2010

I spill out "sorry" more than I breathe
Apologizing again for being upset
At those that hurt me
I always take the blame and bullet

I'm attracted to broken things
The only explanation I have
For not ending things with myself
I am my longest, most toxic relationship

I can't handle the liquor
Stop buying shots for me
This vice that quiets my ruminating thoughts
An evident forewarning

When did "no thanks" mean I'm less fun?
Though I chipped ring, zipper, tooth
Offered coke in a bathroom
For the affirmation of being social

Use introvert as an insult
But I'm in deliberate isolation
A voluntary practice
To protect others from me...

Your wide eyes
Tell me I've said too much again
A reason I struggle to speak
Either a hurricane or a drought
What are boundaries?

Unconsciously you identify me
The Angsty
    Emotional
    Privileged
    Pushover

But what if I'm just
Hurting instead?

The Good Girl's Confession

I am Mother Mary incarnate
Sweet, devout, untouched
A saint toiling amongst sinners

I am introverted
Soaking up the Bible and the world's problems
Every weekend night

I am the hero
With good intentions, no regrets
Saving all from others and themselves

Did I mention
I'm trained in sarcasm
"I'm fine" a useful fabrication

Welcome to my dark side
Hiding in plain sight
All this time

We locked me away
Stuffed into a happy box
A deep-rooted problem with a temporary fix

No escape for processing
So the pressure escalates
Until this vessel implodes

And then they wonder why
I'm
      in
            Shambles

Weird

To be "normal"
That is, to halt the rollercoaster
In my chest and head
Obsessively
Twisting, crumbling
Like my confidence
That ends in doubt
No matter how
Since I'm a contradiction
Overflowing then half empty
Is what I comprehend
Of this spit-worthy nature
I live each day
Of a life that's blessed
Yet cursed
By humanity that
Drags me low...
But what if
I am set ablaze
And remain aglow
Accepting every cell that forms
This body of sensitivity and
Empathy for people
Who don't see me
But fear like a wall
Forbidding me from connection
And getting better
As if something is wrong...
I've come full circle
That what I feel
And who I am
Are two separate beasts
All the while wondering
If I'm truly that different
From those around me.

Mosaic

You introduced me to my favorite band
Seven concerts in six years
Lately I've seen them more than you
So which aspect turned this toxic
My silence or doormat status?

Did I enjoy football
Hustling, running in circles
Of my own accord
Or to be noticed
Deemed enough for your pursuit?

Endured Les Mis in a Czech beret
Football games, the high school across the way
For the halftime that you led
But you hid in the closet
While I steeped in denial

Motorized bikes
Vicious mosh pits
Blackbird singing from your acoustic guitar
Beanie, darkened nails, and sweatbands
Completing my yes-girl attire

Always molded me
To fit the shape I thought you liked
Now how much of me is me
Or simply fragmented pieces
Of you?

Archetype

Do you require assistance?
Your life a perpetual, descending cycle?
Even if you never ask
Don't you fear
Mom friend is here
Consistently providing you

A too eager "yes"
Sustenance
Band-Aids
A hug you must request
Advice no one heeds
A custom of denying her own needs

Mom friend
Uninvited to the bars
Blame her drink limit
And that nervous temperament
She's not the type to let loose
And forget

Mom friend
If invited settles for partial sobriety
Like a guardian saving you
From others with ill intentions
Because the sober see too much
She trusts no one not even herself

Mom friend
Can't ask for support
Never worry
She will never leave
Her self-destructive prescription
All the help that she can give

Mom friend
Unable to comprehend
No one has ever needed her
Since 1995
Pride impersonates selflessness
And insecurity conceals it well.

I Am Your Sunshine
You're only sunshine
I am the one
Chasing the grey skies away

But you'll never know
When the rain falls
If I'm your sun
No part of me is dim

Warped positivity
"Don't worry"
"Be happy"
A grimace mistaken for a grin

False humility makes me forget
That even the sun rests at night
Allowing the moon
To shoulder the world's weight.

The Silent Advocate

Words are my comfort zone
Until they escaped my mind
And suddenly those around me
Heard what goes on inside

I liked the sound of my voice
To use for common good
My words like arrows to negativity
Water dousing fires

But they didn't listen
To my stuttering tongue
That couldn't quite form the thoughts
Cascading, nonstop

I misread the quiet as rejection
Allowing the lies to take root
I am **broken**
Unworthy and **unlovable**

So I settled for silence
Morphed into the persona
Of a shy silhouette
A subdued inferno

Helping, my true motivation
My insufficient offering led me to this
I'll become your little servant instead
By latching my lips.

They Wrote In Report Cards "She Has Leadership Qualities"

Yet she sacrificed these attributes
On the altar of self-hatred
She suppressed their praise
Under fear and people-pleasing
Sought affirmation
In temporary companions
And achievements

Shame ingrained from an early age
Accredit premature puberty
Body jokes she absorbed
Her only craving, popularity
Denied, withheld
Her "good girl" label
A judgment not a compliment

They projected a leader
But instead she cowered
Trapped in the shadow
Of this grand prediction
She heard bossy
And cut herself down
To be adored

I searched for this commander
They harmlessly proposed
But I took it to extremes
Sought to exceed expectations
Until I buried myself in habits
So treacherous
That even their report changed.

Alcoholism Runs In The Family
So I imposed a drinking limit
Two modest alcoholic beverages per sitting
And instantaneously follows
Their smirks and comments
"Lightweight"
As if controlling alcohol's influence
Breeds success
But I digress...
You requested to meet drunk me
Earnestly, repeatedly
Hence two incidents of drunkenness
I gifted you
Opposites as you would expect from me

The first time, unintentional
A condo by the lake
Secure with friends and a boy
A toasted summer breeze
Tequila with a pinch of mix
Fireball's cinnamon graced my lips
Hello carpet, someone's laughing
(It's me)
Something about a board game
Tattling on the werewolf
My face rests on his thigh
Pretty ceiling
Flushed cheeks and giggles
Surely the best day ever

The second time, deliberate
Same companions in their apartment
The eve of a new year, same me
I'm low under winter's wind
And indulge to match their glee
Adult Jell-O, stolen purple wine
Continuous champagne
People cheering, fireworks, cold
Who's that in the mirror
She's weeping
Mascara bleeding on cheeks and hands
(It's me)
Shaking beneath blankets, dissociating
But no blessing of sleep

What if I had not been cradled
In a safe space?
Would strangers respect
An unwary version of me
Or would that despair
Escort me to an early grave?
Flip a coin, 50/50
Blissful drunk/the hopeless kind
A gamble, a risk
I'm not willing to take
Alcohol is nobody's friend
I immediately learned
By the devious manner
It handles me

Understand my limit
Because without it
I'd be swallowed up
In generational curses.

Repress

Declining alcoholic temptation
We bottled our feelings instead
Explode or implode
Spewing anger or never satisfied

Child, pick your poison

The quiet, deliberate burn
The lesser of two evils surely
I ingested the same venom, different label
And no one takes responsibility but me.

Broken Signals

They say "I miss you"
                Then why am I lonely?
If friendship is both give and take
                Why do I sacrifice
And their effort is not the same?

But I never discern
                When to let go
Fixated on shared history
                I can love anyone until they die
Though it's been years since we've spoken
                When I miss someone
I should seek out different company
                And withhold communication
   From those long gone

They say "I care about you"
                But I'm searching for the evidence
Reading between lines
                Memories and past messages
Wondering if I imagined it

But I'm chronically forgetful
                Positive aspects
Slipping from my perspective
                I wallow in yesterday
Instead of who stands
                Right in front of me
I cling to those who left
                Because this end
Isn't proceeded by goodbye

They say "I love you"
    But my brain adds conditions
"If you are
    Useful, happy, thin, sexy
Whatever they decide you to be"

Their declaration hijacked by a lie
That my worth is
    Beauty
    Achievement
    Popularity
    Your expectations of me
And the deeper question lingering
Demanding to be heard
    Does anyone even like me anymore?

With each conflicting message
It's no wonder
    I can't
    Treat me
    Properly.

Dysfunctional Empathy

I gave them all of me
Without boundaries
My gushing heart
Soft soul
Bleeding empathy
Infinite striving
But no impact seen

Once a house of vibrant life
Now   an emptied shell
I drain myself dry
And   never learn
To   receive
To be   nourished
Without   asking

Teach me the   balance
To be   vulnerable
To only the   right people
Without
Emptying
Myself
Entirely.

Punishment

A body shape ideal
I cannot replicate
A number on the scale
That adjusts by the hour
Painted skin
To mark me wished for
But even that flakes away

Beauty becomes
Subjective
Visual
Metamorphic
Unattainable
For the likes of me
I conclude

So I'll shrink further still
Let the front of my stomach
Meet my tailbone
Such a method actor
Feeding the trashcan
A forgotten meal
Halving serving sizes

Innocent intentions that
Boarded the train to disorder
A trip I never planned to take
When I try to starve the mirror and scale
Their words find my ears
Teasing my fragile esteem
"But why? You look so skinny."

Gaslighting

I never needed an adversary
To declare I'm not enough
Assure that I'm invisible
Question my reality
I chose this willingly

I never needed a mean girl
To judge me
Sentencing me **ugly, prude, unlovable**
To shove me to the floor
I took on that duty

I never needed a bully
To crush my lungs
Forget how to breathe
Pound my chest until I can't think or speak
My body gifted this to me

I never needed anyone else
To make me want to die
I only needed me
   Myself
   And I.

Part II
Aftermath

Repression hurts a little less
Than the tsunami of these feelings
Until I bottle them up
And drown in it
Regardless.

Nonstop

Striving
    Petrified of stillness
    The Try-Even-Harder
    Never satisfied

Movement is life
    If I ease this pace
    Secrets concealed
    Will sink their teeth into my brittle shell

Words left unspoken
        Feelings without names
Filling myself with lies in place of nourishment
        Fulfill everyone's demands first
        Reciting yes on all occasions
Toxic independence

Years of destructive routines
        Rejection's sting
Purposeful confinement
        The solution, my salvation
        Eluding my reach
Now where does this leave me?

Ceaselessly fleeing
    The inevitable wave
    Of regret, sorrow, and doubt
    Never knowing
               When
                To
               Stop.

Mania?

The night is on fire
        No, just my skin
Veins pulsing life
        Car chasing its headlights
Windows down
        Forty degrees Fahrenheit

Officer
I promise I've been good
No narcotics
Only a gifted high
My brain hoards
Without remorse

Let me be
I can't waste this elixir
Transforming me
Into a human being
Rise above the grey for a moment
The me of me who doesn't care

Free to make noise
        Take up space
Deliver a speech
        Drive top speed
Sing off-key
        Louder than her heartbeat

        Alive
Winding streets
        Blurring trees
No soul but hers
        Did you know
She could speak?

Engrossed by the music
        Fingers gliding on metallic strings
        Thundering double bass pedal
        Broadway hits with matching motions
        The script of her feelings
        Lyrics branded to her memory

        Buzzing warmth
        Blazing brain to soles
        Catch this flame, this passion
Because sooner than later
It shrinks, tamed
And I'll collide with the ground...

But not quite yet
The sun still beckons
Through the curtains.

I Got That Warm Weather Optimism

So I pretend I'm on a stage
Facing a real crowd
Finally charismatic
Spitting poetry or inspiration
They're laughing with me
Not at my stutter
Or other parts of me that tend to be
The BUTT of the joke

I got that warm weather optimism
I belong behind a steering wheel
Movement is essential
Matching my thoughts' pace
Racing heart and rising chest
But this breath is stuck, trapped
I can't...
Exhale
The wind reminding my lungs of their job

I got that warm weather optimism
I'm suddenly a genius with words
The next F. Scott Fitzgerald
My opinion the talk of the town
Someone is not hearing but listening
Except Francis had a liquor problem
And now I see imaginary faces
Staring, expecting me to deliver
Surely a drink would alleviate this feeling

But the sun is shining
I'm swirling in confident ease
For three hours, a week, a month
Until this morphs into
A hibernation, isolation
Another experiment of stability
I got that warm weather optimism
And for this moment only

                I actually like myself.

The World Is My Stage

Listen as I articulate ideas
I'm so ambitious
Here's my list
Impending accomplishments
It's limitless
I know my purpose
Hopeful, detailing the future
I must share this zeal with anyone
Please listen
It's so profound

But the shower won't magically start
The dishes, laundry, bills
Form a mountain
As I lay on the floor
Forgetting how to breathe
I don't have a reason
What is the purpose?
I'm the finicky type
Idealization all day long
Then I can't find my legs or arms

Where's my brain, there
Spiraling, illogical weights of shame
What's the point?
You can't make a difference
Isolate, be a ghost
Until you're lonely enough
To resurrect
Find affirmation to live again
Only to discover
No one noticed

Persisting in patterns, infinities
Even though I control my destiny
Isn't that what they preached?
I practice self-sabotage
Like it's the sole habit I know
Gaslight my psyche for sport
Maybe I'm not ambitious
And enjoy the comfort of blathering
But I'm on top of the world again
Welcome to my charade

Just wait a few days
And I'll be back on my face.

Self-Mandated Quarantine

There's my cue

Don't have to tell me twice
I'm self-taught in isolation
Perhaps if I ghost the world
They'll notice my disappearance

No one taught me vulnerability
I hide my inner hell inside
Maybe once I am calmed
I'll drag myself back out

A custom of locking myself away
When I become chaotic
Can't articulate what I feel
Alternate between running and hiding

Until the cycle commences...

Swinging up then down, repeat
Fixated, obsessed
Then gnawing emptiness

Double-minded
I demand anyone's attention
Then require nothing

I want to do it all
But I can't do everything
Then aspire to nonexistence

I can't find the truth
"I don't need anyone"
It's you, not me

Then

"I'm saving you from me"
It's not you
But me

But the constant that I can't deny
The wicked part of my brain
Casually whispering

"No one would notice
That you're gone
Anyway."

SAD

Tell me how
I stand on mountaintops
But my mind
Dwells in

Trench.

Little Woman

My secret membership to the sad girls' club
Paid monthly in tears and blood
My closest friends know where I frequent
I assure them "just a bad day"
Or "it's that time of the month"

How did a bad day bleed into years?
Theater taught me well
Display of toothy smiles
Imitation positivity
My stage makeup never smudged

Happiness and usefulness
The recipe of any relationship
"No one wants to be around a sad person"
A mantra to remind my flowing grief
You're not welcome here

Choosing to be liked
Rather than express my feelings
I leech unacceptable emotions
The blatant irony
It only makes me sadder.

Stigma

This little light of mine
I'm gonna let it shine
Precisely, on my hands and eyes
Quite literally
It's vital
In the wintertime

They preach vulnerability
Honesty, what are you feeling?
But I conceal it
As displaying in public places
Only brings the questions
And answers they don't care to know

Explaining to healthy people
Why I own this lamp
I would rather travel towards the sun
Than describe its necessity
Would rather collapse into myself
Than confess my thoughts and habits

"Express your feelings"
"Wait, not like that"
Their response communicates
Anytime I open my mouth to speak
Why not stay silent
If you refuse to hear the truth

I'll hide this little light of mine
Exiled
Ashamed
Because who depends upon an artificial light
To have the will
To live?

Dreamer's Slumber

Welcome to my cage
Where my naivety and I
Dream simply about
Making the world a better place
I unlatch the locks at night
Inspired by the open skies
Thinking of what could be

After years of planning
Strategic survival
I grab my bravery
And burst forth
Believing I prepared
For a successful flight
Effortlessly soaring through the clouds

They cautioned me
"Prepare for the ground"
A safety net
Should this ambition
Lead me to nothing
But I'm too stubborn to forfeit or admit
They are right

My face then body kiss the mud
But nobody moves
They knew this day would come
They have no obligation
So when I cry for help
All that pours out
Is bitterness and self-pity

Doubt crushes my lungs
Still breathing possibilities
Soon replaced by a taunt
"Life owes you nothing
No matter your effort
Or the forecast you deny
They are right"

I clip my wings
Damaged, shrunken things
I lost the longing for flight
I find my feet
A place to cower
And close my eyes
Praying for a changed tomorrow

After the discouragement
They decide to speak the truth
"You can only control your behavior"
Now do you understand
Why this is no longer a slumber
But a
Nightmare?

Unscripted

I would switch it off if I could
The excessive pressure
The endless fluttering
The perpetual flight

Fleeing from distress
I'm attached to a train
Advancing towards a cliff
But never arriving

Relentless productivity, a distraction
In the wake of worry's agenda
Like hell hounds
At my strained heartstrings

I'm not being theatrical
Or maybe that's all there is to this
And that's what terrifies me
How can dramatic hurt this badly?

Surely I'm not playing pretend
The dark cloud isn't imagined
It breeds itself
From fear's persistent attendance

Please bear with me
The cracks in my mask are on full display
I don't like this side of me
The abyss is frightening

Because the darkest shadows
They often
Linger and follow
Don't they?

Intermission: A Panic Attack Waiting In The Wings

What if I can't find a parking spot?
What if I lose my way?
What if I'm late?

What if I stutter in front of a crowd?
What if I lose my train of thought?
What if they think I'm unintelligent?

What if I can't find a job again?
What if I'm stuck in a mind-numbing occupation?
What if nothing ever changes?

What if this bridge breaks
And I drown
Suffocating in my car?

What if there's an earthquake
And this building collapses
Swallowing me whole?

What if someone enters with a gun?
And I can't fight or hide
What if I can't run?

And what if
He doesn't
Come home?

Part III
Regrowth

After the remorseless storm
Denial clings to its last breath
Until Acknowledgement and Acceptance
Put it to rest
And let the healing commence.

Keep Face

Check on your strong friends
Well I'll raise you one more
Check on your happy friends
Those dodging vulnerability
Who wield happiness
As their weapon and shield
To evade the daunting emptiness
Their mind goreshadows

Wary of inauthenticity
But they remain speechless
No one has time to fall apart
Over and over
Life moves forward no matter your mood
Or circumstances aimed to bring you low
The cycle never ceases

Their soundless cries
Appear as laughs and "I'm fine"
How do they unfold the heaviness
That's been escalating for years?
Label it as pride
People-pleasing
Or the fact they never learned
The words to speak about it

Where do I begin
After years of stuffing this down
The only way I know how
I'll fill a book full of words
Everything left unspoken
My most honest confession
I've carried alone for far too long.

Enneagram Type 2, Translation: Low-Key Codependency

Don't you see me?
My hands wide, pleading
For your glance, some attention
A crumb's crumb of affection
I label this love
Yet a cheap replica at best

Giving to receive
Twisted and sick
Disguised manipulation
I steal validation
My thieving cup constantly hollow
Supposedly poor in spirit

For approval
I'll impersonate a helper
To justify my existence
Usefulness makes me worthy
The path to acceptance
I naively embraced

I must separate
My desire to belong
From my willingness to live
And my eagerness to give
No one needs me
And that will have to suffice

I'll surrender my pride
And learn to love myself.

Insecure

Your affirmation is my compass and map
The well I misuse when I feel empty
My reason to stay alive

But that water is detrimental
I become what I think you want
Because I despise every facet of me

A belief told me I am **broken**
And I believe it
The lies burrowing, growing thicker

You became my mirror
For my charming masquerade
A facade parade supplying my vitals

I crave care and acceptance
What I secure is dependency
Depending on others to fill me

My heart leaks anything I receive
And when the validation ceases
My survival method perishes

Then resurrected by a new reason to live
Independent of wants and needs
Any person or worldly thing.

Driftwood

I approach the world so apologetic
I forgot what an apology implies
My posture of blame
Head hung low and bitten tongue
Waiting for the bullet

Insecurity disguised as humility
I let the world's entirety step on me
Docile, repetitive
"I'm sorry"
Begging forgiveness always

My apologies infinite
For expressing anything other than happiness
For my pain when rejected
For having beliefs that contradict yours
Because "it's my fault"

Yet my pinned smile excuses nothing now
I won't play a puppet
The doormat without a door
Here is my proposed boundary
I'm no longer treading silently.

Call Declined

Another winter, another low
I wonder
If he's afraid, ever
Maybe in this moment
Standing in the dining room
Clinging onto me
If he lets go
Will I vanish
Replaced by the images that stalk him?

He's recounted others' experience
Nonchalantly
As if a warning
That can't be my end
These idealizations
Childhood fascinations
Of premature dancing
With my skeleton

Cliff's edge beckoned
Endlessly called for me
He saw the brink
My reckless desires
He held out his hands
And I gave him the blade
An honesty without restraint

Without judgment
Or hopeless pity
He sliced the root of my despair
Dark secrets lose authority
When gifted to the right person
I finally made a good decision

Now I vow to be wholly present
To deny those trains of thought
To remember to live
Even when I drown in feelings
And the day is dark as night

Words are worthless without action
Healing no linear passage
But these graves won't get my bones too soon
I'm too stubborn to surrender

Another day has ended
Here's my gratitude for each breath
That I take for granted

So I'll see you in the morning
I'll see you in the morning

Again;

Defiance

Ten years old, a child
Suffering solitude in a crowded room
At elementary school

Thirteen years
Praying for a death sentence
On a bedroom floor in Suburbia

Eighteen years
Conceding her "best" years
To a college dormitory bed

Twenty-one years
Forfeiting her aspirations
Behind a cash register

Twenty-three years
The darkness she bound
Demanding to be listened to again

Her body fixated
To find itself
Six feet underground

Biographies of writers
Not dictated in their words
Premature deaths by one's own hands

Swinging between shame and sorrow
One detail screams to be heard
Her kind doesn't always last long

The world determined
To rid itself
Of she

But rather she determined
To purge her entirety
Of anything but the Truth

To be or not to be
There is no question
Anymore.

Deceptive Comfort

I've bowed to you
Since the day
I recognized
Thought and feeling
Appointing yourself my
Commander
Prophet
Friend

Restraining
Advising me "no" and "never"
You, my dearest companion
Saving me from danger, certain
"You can't"
"You won't"
And I obeyed you
Forfeiting my plans

But your demands
Conflicting
I'm doubting my doubt
Uneasy in your decreed safety
The chains I shaped
A cell, a tomb
I enclosed with a belief
Believing you knew the Truth

And yet Truth knows who you are
Noise
Deceiver
My enemy
Dear Depression
And Anxiety
I confessed your name aloud
To release your hold on me.

Tender Heart

They designate you weak
Your kind unfit
For the survival of the fittest
Somehow your sweetness
Not a blessing but a curse

Their words latch soul-deep
And you grew ashamed
Of your distinct formation
Fearfully and wonderfully made
It is written in the holy text
Surely not for you

But you provide balance
To their brazen criticism
And infectious apathy
Your empathy a fresh wind
A kindness melting flint souls
Bent on burning the world

Tender Heart
They count you out
And ridicule your tears
But what if this weakness
Makes you the best candidate
For perseverance and strength?

Little One
Don't be fooled
People will call you
Small and short
But you'll hear "insignificant"
And trust it

Shrink to the size they've decided
Shut your lips
Clench your fists
Become a foot mat
A shadow

Little One
Don't get it twisted
Diminishing yourself
Won't make anyone
Less critical, cruel
Or even kind

Hiding never ceased
Innocent but hurtful comments
Yet your quirkiness
And curviness
Never made you any less

Return to the moments
Before the assassination
Of your character
That child-like faith
Where you believed in everyone
Yes, even you

Little One
You're as minuscule
As you allow yourself to be
Small in stature
But tall in spirit.

Canvas

My words create worlds
But a tattered identity
Stole my paintbrush
And illustrated a hellish landscape

My words create worlds
Yet I resigned to a desolate cage
Grasping the keys
Watching the outside world with jealousy

My words create worlds
So I strike the set I established
Disassembled every belief
Hindering me from purpose

My words create my world
I drafted a revised story
Where I'm no longer a character
But a person brimming with grace and mercy

Your words create your world
Don't be deceived like me
But judge and weigh every sentence
That you speak and believe.

Epilogue: Honeycomb Affirmations

So, who am I now...

A glorious temple
> **Adored**
> **Lovely**
> **Precious**

A new creation
> **Accepted**
> **Chosen**
> **Forgiven**

A designed masterpiece
> **Good**
> **Fearfully**
> **And wonderfully made**

A shining beacon
> **Beloved**
> **Worthy**
> **Free**

Who you've always been

> **A child**
> **Of God.**

Made in the USA
Monee, IL
10 September 2021